18th-century English Organ Music

A Graded Anthology

Volume 1

COMPILED AND EDITED BY DAVID PATRICK

MUSIC DEPARTMENT

OXFORD
UNIVERSITY PRESS

OXFORD
UNIVERSITY PRESS

Great Clarendon Street, Oxford OX2 6DP,
United Kingdom

Oxford University Press is a department of the University of Oxford.
It furthers the University's objective of excellence in research, scholarship,
and education by publishing worldwide. Oxford is a registered trade mark of
Oxford University Press in the UK and in certain other countries

First published 2013

Impression: 1

ISBN 978–0–19–338919–9

Music origination by
Enigma Music Production Services, Amersham, Bucks.

Printed in Great Britain on acid-free paper by
Halstan & Co. Ltd, Amersham, Bucks.

CONTENTS

INTRODUCTION

The organ in 18th-century England

The English organ of this period developed in a different way to its counterpart in mainland Europe. In particular, for much of the century the pedal organ did not exist or, if there were pedals, these consisted of 'pull downs' permanently coupled to the Great, as on the organ at Beverly Minster built by John Snetzler (1710–85). It was only late in the century that a rank of individual pedal pipes was added, for example to the organ at St Katherine by the Tower, London, in 1778.

Partly in compensation, the Great and Choir manuals usually extended below the bottom C of organs today, adding low B, B♭, A, G, and sometimes F. Notes in the pieces in this volume which extend beyond the lowest notes of the modern organ may be played an octave higher or omitted (if doubled at the octave) or perhaps played on the pedals using appropriate 16′ stops.

The Swell compass was shorter and only extended down to tenor G or F; passages indicated for Swell would have been accompanied by the left hand on the Choir organ. An enclosed Swell was first introduced by the builder Abraham Jordan in 1712 to the organ at St Magnus the Martyr, London Bridge. This enabled *crescendo* and *diminuendo*, and his innovation was quickly adopted by other builders.

These characteristics gave rise to a particular English repertoire of pieces for manuals only, most notably Cornet and Trumpet voluntaries and Full voluntaries. The first type usually consisted of a short slow movement using Diapasons followed by a quick movement for solo Cornet or Trumpet stop; in some voluntaries the second, quick movement contained quieter passages for the right hand to be played on the Echo or Swell Organ. Full voluntaries had a slow introduction followed by a quicker fugue, both usually played on Full Organ.

Registration

The 18th-century treatises of Jonas Blewitt and John Marsh give detailed rules on registration which may be summarised as follows:

1. The slow introduction found in most voluntaries was played on Open and Stopped Diapasons together (the Open Diapason was never used on its own). Where marked as Swell, this may have implied also using Hautboy.

2. Full Organ consisted of the complete Great Organ, including Mixtures and Reeds but not the Cornet. Sometimes this was qualified by 'with' or 'without' the Trumpet.

3. The Cornet and 8′ Trumpet were used for right-hand solos played on the Great Organ, with the left-hand accompaniment played on the Choir Organ (Stopped Diapason, Flute 4′, and Principal 4′), and echoes played on the Echo or Swell Organ. On the appropriate manual Open and Stopped Diapasons were used to fill out the Great Trumpet and Swell Echo Trumpet. If a solo was played on a Choir reed (Vox Humana, Cremona), the accompaniment was played on the Great Stopped Diapason.

4. The Cornet stop consisted of multiple ranks of Flue pipes, typically 8′, 4′, 2′, 2⅔′ (Twelfth), and 1⅗′ (Tierce). If unavailable, Blewitt reported that the Sesquialtera (generally 1⅗′, 1⅓′, and 1′) was a 'tolerable substitute' in combination with other Flue stops.

5. Passages marked 'Flute' were almost always played on a 4′ stop only, which was found on the Choir Organ and was almost always accompanied by itself (i.e. with the left hand played on the same 4′ Choir stop).

On a typical mid-century instrument, the Great contained the Principal chorus, plus Mixture, Trumpet, and Cornet. The Choir contained the Secondary chorus and possibly secondary reed and Vox Humana. The Swell contained Diapasons and solo stops such as Trumpet and Hautboy.

Ornamentation

The following summary is based on sources of the period.

Appoggiatura
these were used as small-type grace-notes of various note values; in many cases the note value should be interpreted literally, but sometimes a player's judgement is required in order to determine the optimum length.

Beat or mordent
most writers up to the 1750s would have expected the beat or mordent to begin on the lower auxiliary note, thus making a four-note ornament. Thereafter, it became popular as a three-note ornament starting on the main note. However, there is no consistency of interpretation throughout the period.

Trill
sources generally agree that this should begin on the upper note.

Turn
many 18th-century sources described the turn figure as representing the upper-note turn, but some showed these signs as representing an inverted turn. Players should use context to determine the most appropriate interpretation. The turn figure preceded by a short horizontal line should be interpreted as a turn commencing on the main note and taking half of the value of the main note.

Shake ‖ //
generally played as a shake or trill starting on the upper note. It was also used to indicate a lower mordent commencing on the main note.

Bracket
indicates arpeggiation of the chord from the lowest note.

I am grateful to John Collins for his help and advice on these matters.

Cadenzas

Performers in the 18th century would have been expected to add their own cadenza at a chord within a movement that had a pause mark. In this edition, editorial suggestions are given in small type above the right-hand stave; these can be played as they stand, or used as a spur to a player's own invention.

Editorial Method

All items in square brackets, including tempos, accidentals, registration suggestions, and ornaments, are editorial, as are crossed slurs and ties and cue-size notes excluding appoggiaturas. Obvious errors have been corrected without comment; more significant editorial changes are given on p. 60. The marking 'Adagio (ad lib.)' indicated a gradual slowing down to the end of the piece and not a sudden change of pace.

Notes on the Composers

George (Georg) Berg (*c.*1730–*c.*1775) was of German origin and settled in London. He was a violinist and organist and probably studied with J. C. Pepusch (1667–1752); he was elected a member of the Royal Society of Musicians in 1763 and was Organist at Marylebone Gardens until 1769. His compositions include a number of songs and glees and two sets of voluntaries.

Jonas Blewitt (*c.*1757–1805) was almost blind, yet an accomplished player and composer. He was the author of *A Complete Treatise on the Organ*, the first English organ tutor to have been published separately and an important document giving considerable insight into the late 18th-century organ and its registration.

William Boyce (1710–79) was a chorister at St Paul's Cathedral, London, and later an articled pupil of Maurice Greene there. In 1736 he was elected Composer to the Chapel Royal (and Organist from 1758) and in 1755 succeeded Greene as Master of the King's Band. He studied composition under Pepusch and was editor of the three-volume set of *Cathedral Music*, the material for which had been passed to him by Greene.

Charles Burney (1726–1814) was an eminent historian and the author of *A General History of Music* (4 vols., 1776–89). As a composer he studied with Thomas Arne and wrote instrumental music and songs, and held a number of organ posts in London and Norfolk.

Thomas Sanders Dupuis (1733–96) was an Englishman descended from a family of Huguenot refugees. He sang as a treble in the choir of the Chapel Royal, London, and was appointed Organist there in 1779 on the death of William Boyce. A collection of his *Cathedral Music* was published by his pupil John Spencer.

John Garth (*c.*1722–*c.*1810) lived in County Durham, England, and played the organ in the Bishop's Chapel at Auckland Castle.

He was a friend and possibly pupil of Charles Avison, who assisted Garth in the publication of 50 of Benedetto Marcello's *Psalm Paraphrases to English Texts*. Garth was a prolific composer of vocal and instrumental music.

Starling Goodwin (*c.*1713–74) was an organist at several London churches and also Organist of Ranelagh Gardens until 1766. He wrote songs and organ and harpsichord works, as well as *The Complete Organist's Pocket Companion*.

William Goodwin (d. 1784) was probably the son of Starling Goodwin, whom he succeeded as Organist of St Saviour's Southwark, London, in 1774. He was elected a member of the Royal Society of Musicians in 1760, later being expelled, presumably for some misdemeanour. He was one of a number of musicians who performed at London's Ranelagh Gardens.

George Green (fl. *c.*1775) appears to have been an organist in London, but little else is known about his life and work apart from a song 'Neptune's Command', a copy of which is in the British Library. His organ music is typical of voluntaries written in the 1770s.

George Freideric Handel (1685–1759) devised the organ concerto in the mid-1730s, to be played as interludes in performances of his oratorios in Covent Garden, later publishing this set as Op. 4. He also published a 'Second Set' of concertos, the Op. 7 concertos, and *12 Voluntaries and Fugues for the Organ or Harpsichord*.

Henry Heron (*c.*1730–95) was organist of St Magnus the Martyr, London Bridge, from 1762 until his death. His *Ten Voluntaries* are his only published works, though he also wrote a number of songs and ballads for performance at Ranelagh Gardens.

Jacob Kirkman (d. 1812) was Organist at St George's Hanover Square, London. He is possibly one of the Kirkmans who figure in the list of subscribers to Burney's *History of Music* and also likely to be the nephew of another Jacob Kirkman, a famous manufacturer of harpsichords and pianos of the mid-18th century.

Francis Linley (1771–1800) was a practising organist and music dealer, blind from birth. In the early 1790s he purchased Bland's music-selling business, which claimed to be the first music printer to publish singly the works of Handel and other celebrated composers. His compositions include songs, keyboard pieces, some solos and duets for flute, and his organ tutor *A Practical Introduction to the Organ in Five Parts*.

John Marsh (1752–1828), a solicitor by profession, was inspired by the playing of John Stanley and taught himself to play the organ. Some sources suggest he was Assistant Organist at Chichester Cathedral. He arranged many orchestral pieces for the organ and composed a number of original organ pieces.

DAVID PATRICK

June 2013

Voluntary in D
12 Voluntaries for the Organ or Harpsichord, No. 8

WILLIAM GOODWIN (d. 1784)
edited by David Patrick

Voluntary in C major

12 Voluntaries and Fugues for the Organ or Harpsichord, No. 2

attrib. GEORGE FRIDERIC HANDEL (1685–1759)

edited by David Patrick

Andante

[Choir Stopped Diapason, Principal 4']

Voluntary in G minor
Op. 8 No. 16

GEORGE BERG (*c*.1730–*c*.1775)
edited by David Patrick

Voluntary in E♭ major
6 Voluntarys for the Organ, Pianoforte or Harpsichord, No. 1

GEORGE GREEN (fl. *c*.1775)
edited by David Patrick

repeat on the Eccho

Voluntary in C major
9 Voluntaries for the Organ, Set 1 No. 1

THOMAS SANDERS DUPUIS (1733–96)
edited by David Patrick

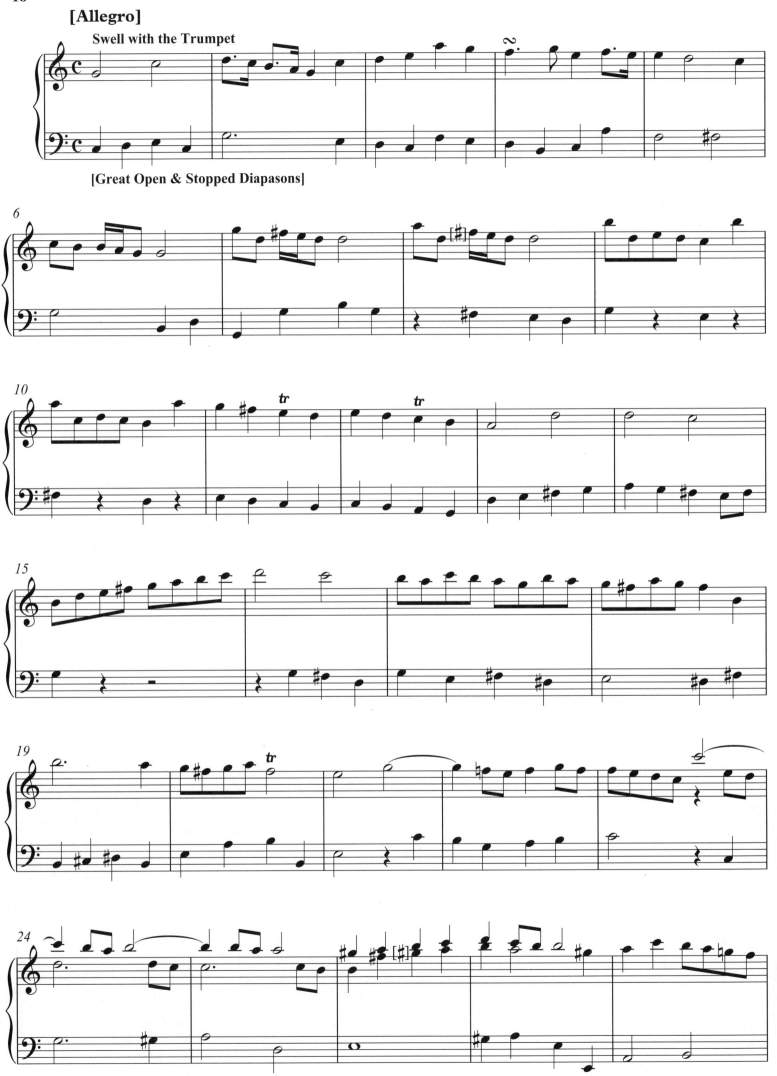

Voluntary in G major
12 Voluntarys for the Organ or Harpsichord, Book 2 No. 1

STARLING GOODWIN (*c.*1713–74)
edited by David Patrick

Fuga

Allegro moderato

Voluntary in A minor
Op. 1 No. 5

HENRY HERON (*c.*1730–95)
edited by David Patrick

[Choir Stopped Diapason, Flute 4', Principal 4']

Voluntary in D
Op. 4 No. 2

JONAS BLEWITT (*c.*1757–1805)
edited by David Patrick

Voluntary in C major
18 Voluntaries for the Organ, No. 1

JOHN MARSH (1752–1828)
edited by David Patrick

Voluntary in G major
12 Voluntarys for the Organ or Harpsichord, Book 2 No. 6

STARLING GOODWIN (*c.*1713–74)
edited by David Patrick

[Allegro]
Cornet

[Choir Open and Stopped Diapasons, Flute 4', Principal 4']

Voluntary in G minor
Op. 2 No. 8

JONAS BLEWITT (*c.*1757–1805)
edited by David Patrick

Siciliano

Swell Diapasons, Principal, Trumpet, and Hautboy

Great Organ Stop Diapason

34

Andante

Vox humane, Cremona or Bassoon

Bass as before

Voluntary in C major
Op. 6 No. 1

FRANCIS LINLEY (1771–1800)
edited by David Patrick

Allegro
Trumpet

[Choir Open and Stopped Diapasons, Flute 4', Principal 4']

Voluntary in E♭ major
Op. 3 No. 4

JOHN GARTH (*c.*1722–*c.*1810)
edited by David Patrick

43

Presto

[Great Diapasons, Principal, Twelfth, Fifteenth, Sesquialtera]

Voluntary in D major
12 Voluntaries and Fugues for the Organ or Harpsichord, No. 10

attrib. GEORGE FRIDERIC HANDEL (1685–1759)
edited by David Patrick

Fugue

Cornet Piece in B minor

6 Cornet Pieces, No. 4

CHARLES BURNEY (1726–1814)

edited by David Patrick

[Choir Open and Stopped Diapasons, Flute 4', Principal 4']

52

Voluntary in C major

10 Voluntaries for the Organ or Harpsichord, No. 6

WILLIAM BOYCE (1710–79)
edited by David Patrick

Voluntary in E♭ major

Op. 9 No. 4

JACOB KIRKMAN (d. 1812)
edited by David Patrick

Maestoso

[Full Organ]

Fugue

Allegro

[Full Organ]

EDITORIAL NOTES AND SOURCES

Editorial Notes

Dupuis, Voluntary in C major:

• [Allegro], b. 35, LH beat 1: D in original, changed to C

Starling Goodwin, Voluntary in G major, Book 2 No. 6:
[Allegro]

• b. 20, LH beat 4: D in original, changed to C
• b. 25, RH beat 3: E in original, changed to D to match b. 126
• b. 121, LH beat 4: C added to match edited b. 20

Green, Voluntary in E♭ major:
Allegro

• b. 3, RH beat 2: semiquavers 2–4 changed from original Ab, G, F to match b. 33
• b. 45, RH beat 2: 4 semiquavers originally a 3rd higher; altered to match bb. 43 and 44
• b. 45, LH beats 3–4: A♭, C in original; probably reversed in error

Handel, Voluntary in D major:

• Spiritoso: demisemiquavers in bb. 1, 2, 4, 5 printed as semiquavers in original

Heron, Voluntary in A minor:

• Adagio: time signature C in original

Linley, Voluntary in C major:

• Moderato, bb. 43 and 45, LH beats 3–4: 2 crotchets in original

Marsh, Voluntary in C major:

• Adagio, b. 2, RH: appoggiatura B also has D 6th below in original
• Largo, b. 47, LH: final semiquaver top part E in original

Sources

Berg: Biblioteca Koninklijk Conservatorium / Conservatoire Royal, Brussels (B-Bc 14048). Ten Voluntaries for the Organ or Harpsichord composed by Mr. George Berg (Opera Ottavo). London, Printed for J. Johnson opposite Bow Church in Cheapside.

Blewitt (Op. 2): London, Royal College of Organists (Sowerbutts Collection). Ten Voluntaries for the Organ or Harpsichord composed by Jonas Blewitt, Organist of St. Catherine Coleman, Fenchurch Street. Opus 2. Printed for the Author by Longman and Broderip, No. 26, Cheapside, London. Music Sellers to the Royal Family.

Blewitt (Op. 4): London, British Library e.120. (1). A Complete Treatise on the Organ to which is added a set of Explanatory Voluntaries composed expressly for the purpose of rendering Theory and Practice subservient to mutual elucidation by Jonas Blewitt. Organist of the united Parishes of St. Margaret Pattens and St. Gabriel Fenchurch. Also of St. Catherine Coleman, Fenchurch Street. Opus 4. Printed by Longman and Broderip, No. 26, Cheapside and No. 13 Haymarket, London.

Boyce: London, British Library e.5.q (1) [c.1785]. 10 Voluntaries for the Organ or Harpsichord composed by the late Dr. William Boyce. London; Printed for S. A. and P. Thompson No. 75 St. Paul's Church Yard.

Burney: London, British Library e.5. (3). VI Cornet Pieces with an Introduction for the Diapasons and a Fugue. Proper for young Organists and Practitioners on the Harpsichord. Compos'd by Mr. Charles Burney. London, Printed for I. Walsh in Catharine Street in the Strand.

Dupuis: London, British Library e.120e [c.1808]. 9 Voluntaries for the Organ composed for the use of Juvenile Organists by the late Doctor Dupuis (Organist to His Majesty). Published by C. Wheatstone, London [c.1808].

Garth: London, British Library d.187. Six Voluntarys for the Organ, Piano Forte or Harpsichord composed by John Garth Opera Terza. Printed by Welcker in Gerrard Street, St. Ann's Soho, London 1771.

Starling Goodwin: London, British Library e.1138e. Twelve Voluntarys for the Organ or Harpsichord composed by Mr. Starling Goodwin late Organist of St. Saviour, Southwark, St. Mary Magdalen, Bermondsey and St. Mary, Newington Butts. Book II. [Probably published by C. and S. Thompson, No. 75, St Paul's Churchyard, London; the title-page has been cropped and no publisher is mentioned.]

William Goodwin: London, British Library d.210.a (1). Twelve Voluntaries for the Organ or Harpsichord composed by William Goodwin, Organist of St. Bartholomew at the Royal Exchange. London. Printed for C. and S. Thompson, No. 75 St. Paul's Church Yard.

Green: London, British Library e.5.h (1*). Six Voluntarys for the Organ, Pianoforte or Harpsichord composed by George Green. London, Printed & sold by Longman, Lukey and Co. No. 26 Cheapside.

Handel: London, British Library e.1089 f. 12 Voluntaries and Fugues for the Organ or Harpsichord with Rules for Tuning by the celebrated Mr. Handel. London, Printed by Longman and Broderip, 26, Cheapside. [c.1780].

Heron: London, British Library d.210 (2). Ten Volentaries [sic] Op.1 for the Organ or Harpsichord composed by Henry Heron, Organist of St. Magnus, London Bridge. Printed for the Author [c.1760].

Kirkman: London, British Library e.120.a (7). A Collection of Six Voluntaries for the Organ, Harpsichord and Piano-forte respectfully dedicated to Miss Margaret Cocks composed by Jacob Kirkman, Organist of St. George's Hanover Square. Opus IX. London. Printed by Longman and Broderip, No. 26 Cheapside and No. 13 Hay Market. Music Sellers and Musical Instrument makers to His Royal Highness the Prince of Wales.

Linley: London, British Library b.330. A Practical Introduction to the Organ in Five Parts viz. A Description of the Organ, Preludes, Voluntarys, Fugues & Full Pieces, and a selection of all the Psalms in General Use with Interludes. Humbly inscribed by permission to Dr. Arnold, Organist & Composer to His Majesty by F. Linley (Op. 6). Twelfth Edition Corrected and Enlarged. London, Wheatstone & Co. 20, Conduit St., Regent Street.

Marsh: London, British Library b.162.a (1). 18 Voluntaries for the Organ. Chiefly intended for the use of Young Practitioners to which is prefixed An Explanation of the different Stops of the Organ & of the several combinations that may be made thereof.—with a few thoughts on style, extempore playing, Modulation etc. London, Preston & Son, Strand 1791.

Complete editions of the Voluntaries by Berg, Blewitt, Burney, Dupuis, Garth, Starling Goodwin, William Goodwin, Green, Kirkman, and Linley are published by Fitzjohn Music Publications (www.impulse-music.co.uk/fitzjohnmusic.htm).